SEDGLEY
& DISTRICT
A FIFTH SELECTION

TREVOR GENGE

SUTTON PUBLISHING

Sutton Publishing Limited
Phoenix Mill · Thrupp · Stroud
Gloucestershire · GL5 2BU

First published 2004

Title page photograph: Sedgley Beacon monument. This mid-twentieth-century postcard shows how the dominating tower and its vantage point remain a landmark so remarkable as to encourage newly created local government, and industries, to incorporate it into the coats of arms of the two urban districts whose boundaries meet at its eastern side. (*Alan Malpass*)

British Library Cataloguing in Publication Data
A catalogue record for this book is available from the British Library.

ISBN 0-7509-3505-7

Typeset in 10.5/13.5 Photina.
Typesetting and origination by Sutton Publishing Limited.
Printed and bound in England by J.H. Haynes & Co. Ltd, Sparkford.

CONTENTS

	Introduction	5
1	Streets, Roads, Lanes & Paths	7
2	Farms	17
3	Houses Great & Small	27
4	Churches & Chapels	35
5	Public Houses	53
6	Schools	59
7	Transport	69
8	Industry	79
9	People & Events	85
10	A Walk Around the Heart of Sedgley	95
11	Epitaph to the Cannon Industries	101
12	History in the Detail	113
	Acknowledgements	127

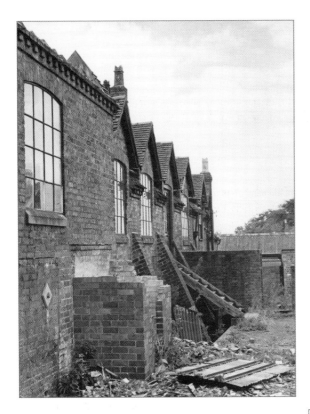

One of the Earl of Dudley's estate yards in 1960. The Earls of Dudley once controlled much of this area and most of its mineral rights. (*Richard Dews*)

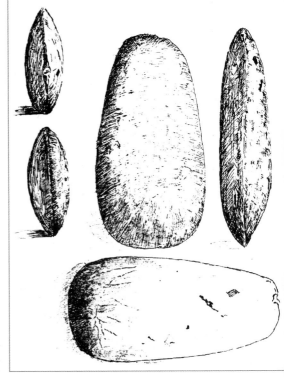

This sketch shows a Stone Age axe head of over 4,000 years ago. It was discovered by Christopher Enright (then aged eleven) in 1984 in a garden in Straits, Lower Gornal, where his grandfather was digging. This is yet a further illustration that the whole of our ancient manor was once a terrain traversed by prehistoric peoples. (*The axe is now kept in the Birmingham City Council Museum and Art Gallery; sketch by F.A. Barnett*)

INTRODUCTION

It is said that the old county of Staffordshire was one of the poorest in England at the time of the Domesday Book. By the eighteenth century, having discovered its wealth beneath the surface, where lay the raw materials to furnish an iron trade, it was one of the richest. Sedgley, Coseley and the two Gornals, together with the other five villages of the parish, sat squarely on the eastern beds of these sources of wealth.

Although the extraction of minerals and the heavy industry it fed scarred the landscape and to many of its people led to the 'bad old days', a community spirit evolved, and continues to exist today, particularly in the older areas.

This second book in the Sedgley, Coseley and the Gornals series is the fifth (if one includes the Sedgley and District titles). It would seem that along with that once prolific mineral wealth a fund of memories and records has accumulated and can still be mined, including a wonderful photographic record. Once again people's individual treasures have been loaned to assist in the creation of this new record of Black Country life.

Most memories are precious, if not always fond, and many speak of the pride and the resilience of this area. Sedgley, Coseley and the Gornals are not without their wounds, particularly those inflicted by the twentieth-century loss of their heavy industries and firms with household names that once spanned the globe. Especially featured in this book is the Cannon, famed for its gas fires, cookers and a host of other products, many forgotten; its last small department, at Deepfields, closed on 28 March 2003, after a history dating back to 1826.

This book also reminds us of that even earlier history and the echoes of that once 'green and pleasant land' still visible among both old despoliation and modern development. It also remembers its people, some known locally for their work, others for their contribution to early local government, particularly during the first years of the two urban districts that succeeded the parish. The local schools, churches, shops and pubs of the area are also visited, and aspects of their life remembered. Forgotten streetscapes re-emerge, and the transport used to reach them or by which people escaped from them, if only temporarily. Wherever possible each of the nine villages is represented. While each village name has evolved over the years, all nine are recorded in a significant land deed of 1614.

Sedgley itself was obviously present before the Domesday Book of 1086, as was Bradley, before its division into the two halves of Bradley in Bilston and Brierley in

Sedgley. The name Gornal is of Old English derivation, meaning a (water) mill in a low-lying, possibly hidden nook, of the landscape. There is a distinct possibility that the area existed as a whole before the prefixes of Upper (Ouvre) or Lower (Nether) were added. Its eastern boundary might even have enclosed part of the land now recognised as Woodsetton. Coseley appears to get its first reference in 1292, in an inventory recorded by John S. Roper MA; but how long the name had been in local usage before is not known.

I have tried to shows examples of beneficial change as well as regretted change, and some commendable restorations of old buildings too, sometimes with the aid of 'then and now' photographs to refresh the memory and to create a permanent record of our vanishing past. Space is also found here for the ongoing work of investigating the past, for the recording of heritage, so that this knowledge will be preserved for the future.

Not all the illustrations are photographic: some pages reveal the talent of our local artist historians. There are also long-forgotten advertisements to jog the memory and to be cause for conversation. There are important documents and letters showing occasions and events remembered by some and worthy of record.

I am, as always, indebted to the many people who have helped in however small a way in the creation of this book, and for their accompanying memories, though no doubt some may recall them differently.

1

Streets, Roads, Lanes & Paths

The old field path and bier way from Sedgley Hall to All Saints' Church in winter, 1980s. The stub of one stone post of a stile can be seen on the right. (*F.A. Barnett*)

The last of the elms of Catholic Lane, believed to have been planted as an avenue by the Caswell family, local farmers. (*F.A. Barnett*)

A winter scene where Moden Hill Lane approaches the entrance to the north drive of Ellowes Hall. The rugged stone post by the concrete lamp standard is the old village boundary marker: Cotwall End is to the west, Sedgley lies north, and Upper Gornal to the south. (*F.A. Barnett*)

Two 1940s postcard views. The top picture, taken near the entrance to Gate Street, looks south to the elegant houses of the late nineteenth-/early twentieth-century development of High Holborn: note the tramlines still in evidence. (*George Cox*) The bottom picture looks north down Dudley Street, showing Cartwright's newsagents on the left. Beyond is the Pound and Knight's, the little single-storeyed tobacconist's (beyond the trolley bus post), while the Clifton cinema stands at the rear. On the right are the old houses that in time became the shops of the present street. (*Alan Malpass*)

The Birmingham New Road, looking south, shows the trees in their splendour in 1985. The photograph was taken shortly before the removal of some of the trees, on the eastern side, near Meadow Lane, to provide an entrance for a new link road to the Black Country route travelling east to join the M6 motorway at Junction 10. (*Trevor Genge*)

This picture shows the road to the north of Lanesfield in 1994 cutting through old, disturbed, land levels on its way to Parkfield and the city of Wolverhampton. Mid-twentieth-century housing stands on the brows of previous rolling banks where masses of wildflowers bloomed, having re-established themselves from an area of small pits and their attendant spoil heaps. (*Trevor Genge*)

Traditional scenes of an ancient manor still resist change. The view down Catholic Lane in autumn 1968 while showing the preparation of a car park for the Cotwall End Nature Reserve (now Critta's Farm), still provides a view looked over for many years. (*F.A. Barnett*)

This fine view, looking north across Adder's Piece to houses in Catholic Lane in 1975, is from Moden Hill Lane. It fully deserves the description of 'rural'. Yet a working gin pit colliery, Williams's, flourished not a quarter of a mile away, into the second half of the twentieth century (*F.A. Barnett*)

The remains of an old track that ran from Duke Street to an area in Ruiton, in Upper Gornal, known as Botany, and continued onwards to Moden Hill. (*Trevor Genge*)

An old field path in Upper Gornal in the snow. The path ran behind the Cottage of Content, and sadly lost its stile after 1965. (*F.A. Barnett*)

Fine views are afforded on either side of the Sedgley Ridge. The view west from Duke Street, Upper Gornal looks beyond Shropshire towards Montgomeryshire – a benefit for many local dwellers, presenting an ever changing picture as time and the seasons pass. (*Trevor Genge*)

ake Street, Lower Gornal, as it proceeds southwards towards the old hamlet of Deepdale Bank. The focal oint of the hamlet is the pub, which can be seen prominently on the bank on the right. (*Trevor Genge*)

The Black Bear

Church Road in Coseley is now a quiet backwater close to Christ Church, which was consecrated in 1830; its lych gate can be seen here. With its school and vicarage close by, the street embodies the image of an ideal village settlement in this once heavily industrialised locality. The nearby cricket ground is on land once part of the Paddock Colliery site. (*E.A. Barnett*)

The Broadway was created in 1937 from Dudley town to Upper Gornal through the lands of the old village of Woodsetton, in which the castle stands. Though providing a useful through road for Birmingham, to the south and east, without passing through Dudley town centre, its main objective seems to have been to provide access to new housing developments, the Priory estate and others on either side. (*John Grainger Collection*)

This scene looking north down Havacre Lane, Coseley, in the 1970s still shows its entitlement to the description 'lane', in striking contrast to a modern road. It winds its way from the railway station and onwards to Deepfields where it meets the equally winding Coseley Road from Bilston. (*F.A. Barnett*)

2

Farms

A glimpse of the fields behind Wood Farm, on the Cotwall End/Gospel End border. The recorded history of these fields goes back 700 years, to the time of one Moysi the Forester. (*Trevor Genge*)

Abbey Farm, Lower Gornal, was pictured on page 20 of book 1. It stood in the heart of Gornal Wood, where some of the streets are still referred to as the Meadow and Barr's Meadow. This eighteenth-century farm house was being demolished in 1966. (*F.A. Barnett*)

Looking east, probably in the early 1970s. The Ellowes School rises within the lands of the previously demolished mansion of Ellowes Hall. The fields are in Cotwall End, looking across Calves Croft in the foreground, where the harvest has been gathered. (*F.A. Barnett*)

A harvest of mangel wurzels, or sugar beet, being gathered at Spout House Farm, 1960s. The man with the cap on the left is thought to be farmer Reg Whitmore. The tractor is probably an early Ferguson, originally supplied without a cab – the cab shown here was probably made at the farm. (*F.A. Barnett*)

The white-gabled Spout House Farm stands in the distance surrounded by fields with protective fencing for the North Sea gas pipelines in 1972. (*F.A. Barnett*)

SEDGLEY BEACON FROM THE EAST.   RON BAKER

A sketch by Ron Baker after Andrew Barnett, showing Sedgley Beacon from the east with its tower dominating the horizon, *c.* 1925. Sedgley Beacon was ploughed to the top from Ettingshall Park Farm. The horses usually ploughed north to south. This picture illustrates the typical variations of land use in the Black Country. To the left of the picture is a section of the hamlet of Cinder Hill, the Talbot Inn on the left, Homer's Barn (see book 4, page 20) already ruinous, and a glimpse of houses in what was known as Pantry

Row peeping from behind the barn. In the middle ground are brick drying sheds, belonging to an almost forgotten brickworks. In 1904 a Mr I. Hughes was the proprietor, and to the right stands the house of the Rudge family. In the foreground haymaking is in progress by the fenced Lower Path, which leads from Ettingshall to Sedgley. Although useful to workmen returning from the factories, this path was part of an ancient bier way, along which many a coffin was carried to All Saints' Church. (*Ron Baker after F.A. Barnett*)

A summer scene showing Sandyfields Farm and buildings, in Cotwall End, 1976. Another of our persistent survivals, it stands on an ancient bend in the road now reduced to a service road having been straightened. (*Trevor Genge*)

Another summer scene, with the winding Moden Hill Lane climbing the ridge of the Russell's Hall fault. The fields were once part of the Ellowes Hall estate, and the tree-lined Ellowes Drive can be seen here. The little white cottage centre left can be seen on page 33. (*F.A. Barnett*)

The village lands of Cotwall End and Gospel End meet on either side of Dyg Lane. Above the late twentieth-century private stables, in the middle, some of the buildings of Wood Farm can be seen. It is probable that there has been a house on this site since the second half of the thirteenth century. (*Trevor Genge*)

An extensive brick barn with dovecote, with an entrance for the hay wain, *c.* 1960. Once part of Wood Farm, it has now been converted to a private residence. (*Trevor Genge*)

Red Lane Farm at harvest time in the 1930s when corn was placed in stooks, and horses provided the horse power. These scenes show the Nickolds family at work and play. The curly haired youngster is Laurence Nickolds, the present farmer. (*Laurence Nickolds*)

This covered spring in Lower Gornal is an old remnant of village life. One of its names, Sugar Well, suggests an additional flavour to the water, but in some parts of the country an alternative meaning is Robbers' Well. (*F.A. Barnett*)

The name Harvest Home brings to mind the work of the miller, and the stump of Ruiton's second windmill still provides one of the dominating features of the skyline. 'Ruiton' means 'Rye farm', a reminder that from the earliest times, when water mills were in use, until the use of wind mills, rye was one of the main cereal crops grown in local fields. (*Trevor Genge*)

3

Houses Great & Small

The survivor! This is the only remaining house in Field Street. Situated just within Brierley/Bradley village, in old Sedgley parish and near the boundary with Bilston, it has survived thus far (2003) as office accommodation. (*Trevor Genge*)

Old Hermit Row with Ruiton Congregational Church beyond. Ruiton is the old heart of Upper Gornal village, and roads radiate in several directions from the church gates. (*F.A. Barnett*)

The buildings on the right were put to many uses, including nail-making, before they finally fell into decay, as shown here in these *c.* 1980 photographs of Vale Street, Ruiton, Upper Gornal. (*Trevor Genge*)

This building has a hatch in the upper storey through which materials could be raised or lowered. (*Trevor Genge*)

Here are the same buildings today commendably restored and converted into a fine house. (*Trevor Genge*)

This house in Straits Road, Lower Gornal, was demolished in 2003 to make way for a modern house. It was one of several, locally built houses that followed the principle of having the windows and doors in the front elevation only, with its back turned to the road. The red sandstone used in its construction was from the vicinity of Straits Green and Gordon's Place. (*Trevor Genge*)

The houses by the mill in Vale Street, Ruiton, Upper Gornal. Note the double stack of the building and in particular its length, which suggests that it was originally a mill house built in the style of a farm 'long house', where man and animals were accommodated under one roof. (*Trevor Genge*)

Ruiton House in Vale Street dates back at least to the eighteenth century. (*Trevor Genge*)

This white cottage stands high on Moden Hill Lane, although it is in fact in Cotwall End, not quite in Upper Gornal. It is one of the few remaining local examples of domestic building in stone after 1850, and is shown on the Sedgley tithe map of 1843. (*Trevor Genge*)

These late 1920s council houses in Ward Grove, Lanesfield, were built by Coseley Council in response to the 'Homes fit for Heroes' scheme following the First World War. They are shown here in about 1975, before refurbishment. (*Trevor Genge*)

These houses show the local love of ornamentation and ostentation. Hurst Hill House stands in Clifton Street formerly Hurst Hill Street, while Belmont Cottages (1906) stand in Spring Road/Manor Road, Lanesfield Though not close to each other they both fell within the boundaries of Ettingshall village. (*Trevor Genge*)

4

Churches & Chapels

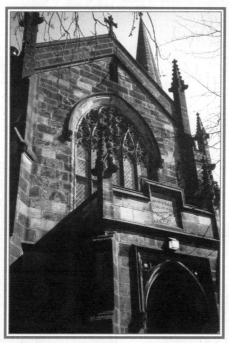

The dedication to John William, Earl of Dudley, above the entrance door to All Saints', Sedgley's parish church, marking the year of rebuilding, 1829. A priest is recorded here in the Domesday Book of 1086, though an earlier church might have occupied this site before Domesday. The year 2004 will celebrate the 175th anniversary of the new building. (*Trevor Genge*)

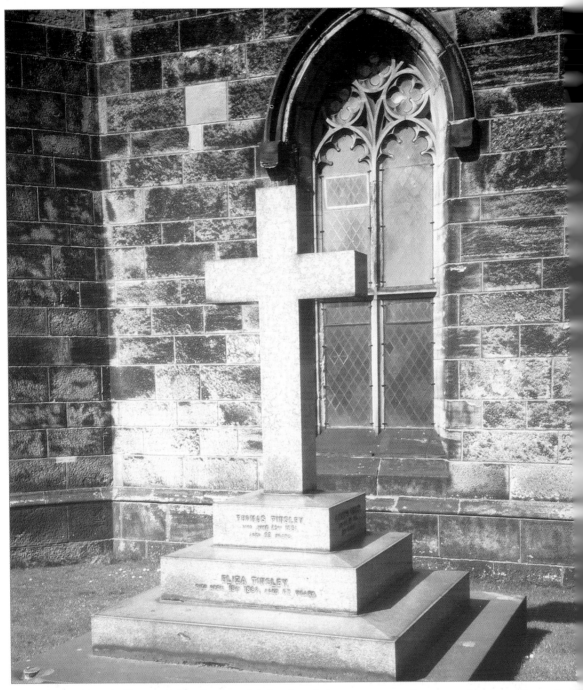

To the south side of All Saints' Church is a reminder that the area was once the scene of an extensive cottage nail-making industry. The cross marks the grave of the Tinsley family, nail factors, most remembered for Thomas Tinsley's widow Eliza, whose empire stretched through Dudley and as far south as Bromsgrove. Living at The Limes in Upper Gornal, she became a local celebrity on her husband's death – for having dared to take up the challenge of continuing his business – and her name appears on several foundation stones and old charitable subscription lists. The name is maintained in industry to this day. (*Trevor Genge*)

All Saints' bell ringers, 1948. Clockwise from front left: Alan Malpass, Billy Mills, Sid Jennings, Wilf Fullwood, Billy Lowe, Alf Abbas, Ben Fullwood, Ernie Barratt. (*Alan Malpass*)

An Armistice day parade leaves All Saints' on 11 November 1950, and marches along Vicar Street, passing the old vestry room, scene of the first Board of Health meetings. A dignitary taking the salute stands in front of the 1808 graveyard, the building of which meant that Vicar Street had to be made a through road joining Dudley Street with Gospel End Street. (*Alan Malpass*)

An engraving of *c.* 1900 showing Sedgley Congregational Chapel in Bilston Street. The Darbey Day School stands to the left. The caretaker's house can still be seen in between. (*Trevor Genge*)

This engraving of the chapel in 1916 shows the box pews, central pulpit and ornamental gas pipes typical of the period. The gallery and organ loft were later additions to the original church, and were undertaken by Hilton and Caswell, whose house and yard were prominently placed in the Bull Ring. (*Trevor Genge*)

After the 1970 union between the Bilston Street Congregationalists and the High Street Methodists there was increasing demand for space for the meetings of both churches. An early measure was the erection of a wooden building, which is here being officially opened. The Revd Brian O'Gorman, chairman of the Methodist District, turns the key in the lock, watched by Reverend Jim Mc'Wade (minister), the Reverend Maurice Hussellbee, Congregational Moderator, and two members of the congregation, Richard Price and Richard Jordan. (*Trevor Genge*)

One of the features in the early life of the newly formed church of St Andrew's was the formation of the St Andrew's Singers, seen here in 1973. Back row, left to right: Margaret Noakes (conductor), Norma Tilt, Brenda Walton, Grace Watkins, Rita Forrest, Barbara Gelsthorpe, Jean Hodgkiss. Front row: Margaret Peters, June Evans, Shelagh Barker, Sue Giles, Lorraine Beardsmore, Jean Darlington (pianist). (*Trevor Genge*)

The churches often provided recreation as well as a place of worship. This group consists of members of the Hurst Hill Methodist Tennis and Croquet Club, *c.* 1925. (*Gladys Thomas*)

The Whitehead family on a Hurst Hill church outing to New Brighton pose for a seaside photograph, *c.* 1920. (*Gladys Thomas*)

Providence Baptist Church and Sunday school, *c.* 1965, now demolished. The Sunday school on the right had been the earlier church of 1809. The later church, to the left behind the trees, had its roof lowered and the gallery removed during the last decades of the twentieth century. Remodelling of the lower storey has since taken place and extensions added to compensate for the loss of space. (*Andrew Barnett Collection*)

Mount Tabor Methodist Church in Woodsetton, fronted by the local war memorial. The church has now closed for worship, and the building is used for light industrial activity. (*Trevor Genge*)

Youth clubs and Sunday schools flourished in the years following the Second World War. Here are Hurst Hill Methodist Sunday school leaders and staff in 1953. Their minister is the Revd Arthur Connop. (*Gladys Thomas*)

All Saints' Girl Guides parade to church along Tipton Street, Sedgley, *c.* 1935. (*George Cox*)

Lanesfield carnival, *c.* 1953. The Youth Club's lunar float is a reminder of the increased interest in space exploration at the time. Pilot, travel agents and passengers include Edward Mason, Pat Thickbroom, Sue Genge, Brian Lewis, Betty Ellis, Michael Clews, Margaret Davis and Alma Price. (*Margaret Genge*)

Lanesfield Youth Club, *c.* 1960. The club's leader Norman Smith stands at the rear. The assistant leader is Ernie Noakes (in tracksuit seated at the front). (*Cecil and Dorothy Baines*)

All Saints' Children's Festival parade, 1934, led by the 1st Sedgley Scouts. (*George Cox*)

The Sunday school outing was an important annual landmark. Here High Street Methodists, Sedgley district, pose on the tiered steps for a group photograph of the 1950s. (*Doreen Thompson*)

Sedgley's history is a constant source of interest to local people. Here, in the summer of 2003, Christine Buckley, wife of the Revd Stephen Buckley, vicar of All Saints', seizes an opportunity for archaeological exploration when the removal of a recent floor covering allowed access to the site of the previous church beneath. (*Trevor Genge*)

The traditional three steps of the base of the old village preaching cross, thought to be of fourteenth-century date, were moved, possibly at the time of the new church building between 1826 and 1829, to the graveyard in Gospel End Street. (*Trevor Genge*)

The church of St James, Lower Gornal, held a three-day bazaar in 1932 to cover the outstanding debts from the building of the memorial hall. The hall, funded by public subscription, was to provide improved teaching facilities (since the old school house was proving inadequate) and an assembly hall for church use. It was opened in 1929. So important was the event to the parish of Lower Gornal that the Bishop of Lichfield wrote a message of greeting for inclusion in the programme. (*Vi Marsh*)

DAN FIELD,

FIVE WAYS,
Lower Gornal

has a reputation for Best English Home Killed Beef, Veal, Mutton, Lamb, and Pork. English Home Cured Hams & Bacon a speciality.

All below Town Prices.

Customers called on Daily —Prompt Delivery.

Established at the above address for over 30 years.

Local shops and businesses advertised in the fund-raising programme. Dan Field, local butcher, was one of them. The advert refers to his history of thirty years as a butcher at the Five Ways. Field's business expanded until he had shops in Lower Gornal and Sedgley; the firm has recently celebrated its centenary. (*Vi Marsh*)

A typical nonconformist Sunday school anniversary performance. Here is the Sunday school anniversary choir at Himley Road Methodist Church. The platform is traditionally arranged, with the adult choir at the rear, the Sunday school children at the front, ranked by age and dressed in white, and the organist, leader and participating ministers completing the scene. This photograph was taken in the late 1950s or early 1960s. (*Vi Marsh*)

A choir outing from Hurst Hill Chapel, 1925. (*Gladys Thomas*)

Ruiton Congregational Church, Hermit Street (seen on pages 28 and 29), behind old Hermit Row. The interior of this 174-year-old church now has a modern, light and cared-for look. (*Ron Williams*)

5

Public Houses

The Grand Junction Inn, Sedgley, situated on the corner of Tipton Street and High Holborn. The building has changed little over the years. Built in stone, it has seven windows blocked up – to avoid payment of the 1851 window tax – and another extended to provide light on two floors. There are stables and coach house buildings in the yard at the rear. (*Trevor Genge*)

The Swan Inn, Gospel End Street, is one of Sedgley's older inns; it is seen here in 2000. One can clearly see how over the years the building has been extended from an original smaller house. The piece of land on the east side, best remembered as the site of a large advertising hoarding, was used previously by J.T. Homer for a 'tin mission' to provide a centre of worship after he had sold his father's temperance hall, in the High Street (see *Sedgley & District* book 1, page 72). The land, now cleared, is grassed and maintained as a children's play space. (*Trevor Genge*)

The Rollers Arms, Foundry Street, Coseley (Darkhouse, 2000) recalls a time when many of its customers would have worked in the local rolling mills that belonged to the local foundry and heavy industries that predominated in this area. Characteristically, this building suffers from undermining, and so the south wall has significant brick buttresses. (*Trevor Genge*)

The first of these two photographs of the Britannia Inn, Kent Street, Upper Gornal, appeared in *Sedgley & District* book 1 as an inn that developed from a single cottage, gaining a licence as a beer house around 1832. It is seen here with a twentieth-century LaserJet advert, revealing the state and dilapidation the passage of time had brought to it. (*Dudley Archives and Local History Service*) The photograph below shows the inn as it appears today after a recent, sympathetic restoration. Little if any of its original character has been lost and the streetscape also remains unaltered. (*Trevor Genge*)

The Pig on the Wall, Kent Street, Upper Gornal, 2002. It had previously been the Bricklayers Arms, shown in the first *Sedgley, Coseley and the Gornals*, when Harry Hammond was landlord. The Pig on the Wall refers to a popular Gornal story of a pig whose front legs were lifted to the top of a roadside wall to watch and enjoy a local brass band going by. The pub soon became a popular eating place too, a successful transition made by many local public houses. (*Trevor Genge*)

Many complaints were voiced when the Pig on the Wall was demolished in the late autumn of 2002 and the land developed by this well-known food outlet. The building was constructed rapidly, opening before Christmas. (*Trevor Genge*)

The Crown Inn, Ruiton, Upper Gornal, with its double stack construction. Ruiton hamlet was probably the ancient centre of Upper Gornal village, and the Crown Inn, dating from the early nineteenth century or earlier, stands just in Vale Street, opposite the Congregational Chapel. The wide spaciousness created by the entrances to Hermit Street, Holloway Street, Duke Street, and Vale Street gives the impression of what might once have been a village green and, in harsher times, even the site of a bull ring. (*Trevor Genge*)

The Globe Inn in Brierley/Bradley stands at the corner of Lane Street and Ash Street. While being a casualty of the recent decline in the public house trade – as a result of competition with fast-food establishments and the availability of alcohol in supermarkets for home consumption – the building has not been lost, and its name board remains as the means of advertising its new function as a paint supplier. (*Trevor Genge*)

The Summer House, Gospel End, lying well back from the Gospel End Road, *c.* 1975. Serving the surrounding village community and outlying farms and cottages, the Summer House existed long before the road was surfaced. Its closeness to a now culverted stream suggests the possibility of in-house brewing. Its name may be a corruption of 'sumpter', the name given to early transporters of local nails and iron goods from Sedgley to Bewdley for export. Once the word for the panniers astride the mules' or donkeys' backs, it became the term for the drivers themselves, who may well have availed themselves of a drink during their long journeys to and fro. (*Trevor Genge*)

The Lion Inn, Kent Street, Upper Gornal, *c.* 1911. This Kent Street house was one of the many casualties of redevelopment, particularly along the east side of the road. The arch entrance provided an extra bedroom for the inn and joined it to the Kent Street Wesley caretaker's house, while the chapel itself was next door. The arch provided access to the Sunday school at the rear, avoiding the need to go through the chapel. Here are Ada Elizabeth Cartwright (in the white blouse, left), Ada's youngest brother, Jim Colbourne, and Leah Rowlinson (the maid), who was sadly to commit suicide. One of the men looking through the window is Ada's father. (*Lyn Suvanto*)

6

Schools

Sedgley School Board foundation stone, Mount Pleasant School, Coseley. In the years
following the Education Act of 1870, when churches, chapels and other charitable
donors initiated an 'education for all' policy, there were still not enough schools, so
local boards tried to fill the vacuum. Many local schools were built under the
auspices of Sedgley Board, and were popularly known as Board Schools. The names
on local foundation stones reveal the prominent citizens involved in the initiatives.
(*F.A. Barnett*)

The Broad Lanes Tin School, Ladymoor, 1921. This school survived into the twentieth century, when it gave way to the Broadlanes Elementary and Senior Schools, which in turn were demolished in 2002. This drawing is by Andrew Barnett, a former pupil who later became head teacher at Red Hall, Lower Gornal. (*F.A. Barnett*)

Opposite: A teacher leads a group of children from Red Hall Juniors through a quiet backwater of Gornal Wood, Lower Gornal, *c.* 1960. Where a neighbourhood is proud of its past, as Gornal is, it is not surprising that it always teaches the young how to respect and enjoy its history. (*F.A. Barnett*)

The staff of Broadlanes Senior School, mid-1950s. Back row, left to right: Reg Counter, Derwyn Davies, ? Davies, Jeff Martin, Gerald Hart. Middle row: Bill Boast, ? Gulliver, Les Clark, Fred Crump, Don Perry, Alan Penn. Front row: Gwen Lang (School Secretary), Olga Crump, Annie Stansfield (Deputy Head), Leonard Jackson (Headmaster), Collin Hopcutt, Elsie Barnett, Rena Rowlands. (*Annie Stansfield*)

Lanesfield Primary School's meadow, May 1988. This new school replaced the old Wood Street School, and recreated the countryside in its own way by creating a wildflower meadow in the school grounds. (*Trevor Genge*)

Headmaster Leonard Wearing and staff enjoying an informal moment after hours at Wood Street School, Lanesfield, 1961. School secretary Lily Gowand can be seen at the back left of the photograph. (*Lanesfield Primary School*)

Wood Street School was always noted for its plays and other dramatic performances to which parents were invited. Here the cast of one of those performances gathers in full costume on the school playground, *c.* 1950, for a production set in the countryside, so different from the environment in which the school stood.

VEGETABLE PRODUCTS COMMITTEE
FOR NAVAL SUPPLY.

Central Depot :--SALVAGE WAREHOUSE, PADDINGTON GOODS STATION, LONDON.

PATRON : **H.M. THE KING.**
PRESIDENT :
ADMIRAL THE LORD BERESFORD,
G.C.B., etc.

HONORARY DIRECTOR :
E. JEROME DYER, O.B.E.

TEL : REGENT 5685.
TELEGRAPHIC ADDRESS :
"MINEURS, LONDON."

REGISTERED PURSUANT TO THE
WAR CHARITIES ACT, 1916.

Head Offices :--46, DOVER STREET,
PICCADILLY,
LONDON, W.1.

November 11th 1919

To/
    Master Arthur Woodfield,
      R. C. School,
        Sedgley.

Dear Master Arthur,

    Following on the records and testimony of Mrs. J. Brown
the highly esteemed Honorary Secretary of our Sedgley Branch,
I am request by the Central Executive of this Organisation,
to certify that you have rendered consistent and valuable
voluntary assistance in supplying the gallant sailors of our
Navy with gifts of fresh vegetables and fruit for their health
and comfort during the Great War which started on August 4th,
1914.

    We not only desire to testify our own sincere esteem of
your generous and patriotic co-operation, but by authority of
Admiral of the Fleet - Lord Beatty we have great pleasure in
conveying to you the hearty thanks and appreciation of the
Fleet.

                Yours faithfully,

                    [signature]

QB.
                     Honorary Director.

A fascinating letter sent to Arthur Woodfield, a pupil of St Chad's Roman Catholic School, High Holborn, Sedgley, in 1919, acknowledging a gift. A department associated with the Admiralty thanked him for his efforts in providing fresh vegetables and fruit for the sailors during the First World War. (*Ron Baker*)

Girls' netball team, Bramford Primary School, Woodsetton, mid-1970s. Fran Plane (née Jevons) is their teacher, standing to the left. Back row, left to right: Jayne Pearce, Kathryn Wasdell, Karen Halford, Tina Jones, Vicky Cook. Front row: Loraine Smart, Julie Smart, Maurene Hutchinson, Helen ? (*Trevor Genge*)

Standard 8 Class, Hurst Hill School, *c.* 1920. Back row, left to right: Gwen Milne, Reg Turley, Harold Follows, Sammy Jones, Sam Caddick, William Edwards. Middle row: Doris Millard, Muriel Adams, Annie

Smith, Peggy Bailey. The Headmaster is T.B. Davies and to his left Jimmy Webb and to his right Arthur Richards. Front row: Ken Nicholls, Leslie Jones, Billy Gough, Howard Slater. (*Iris Turley*)

Alder Coppice Primary School, on an archaeological dig on the site of Sedgley Hall farm, 1971. The pupils were assisted by staff and students from Wolverhampton Teachers Day College. The school and the children's houses were mostly built on former farmland, many of which had belonged to the Hall. (*Trevor Genge*)

Here is the moment when the old kitchen quarry tiles were uncovered! A halfpenny (dated 1851) followed soon afterwards, and much discussion ensued: was it buried to mark the construction of the building, or was it dropped accidentally some time later? (*Trevor Genge*)

7

Transport

By rail to nowhere? The disused line of the old railway serving Gornal Halt and some of the Earl of Dudley's freight movements cuts a sad picture, a sign of change in both local transport and industry, after the line's closure in 1965. (*E. Fanks*)

Above: Brindley's eighteenth-century canal at Highfields, looking south. The widened basin at this point served a coal yard, but years earlier Stephen Thompson moved his enterprise around the canal to the new Ettingshall Village to begin his boiler works, which was to grow into the great John Thompson empire. Thompson couldn't have known that in the future it would provide employment for thousands in its many companies. The public house in the distance was the Boat, at Highfields. Another Boat Inn can be found at Deepfields. The inn pictured here in 1970 was vacated and burned down shortly after this picture was taken. (*Author's Collection*) *Below*: the new Highfields Bridge, from Rainbow Street, with the Boat Inn seen from the other side. (*F.A. Barnett*)

The old branch of the Brindley canal to the Cannon and to Henry Bickerton Whitehouse's furnaces was included in the new Telford main line of the 1830s. The bridges have a grace of their own and here provide a framed glimpse of Matty's boat yard beyond. Both photographs date from about 1970. (*Ray Whitehouse*)

A close-up of Matty's boat yard. An old wooden boat tied to the bank may be due for conversion from a working boat to a leisure craft. (*Author's Collection*) The picture below, a view from Ivy House Lane towards Deepfields, is from above the north portal of Telford's Coseley Tunnel. The Deepfields footbridge is still in place. Originally its main purpose was to provide a 'coffin way' to All Saints', Sedgley, necessary before Christ Church, Coseley, was built in 1830. Coseley School, opened in November 1969, can be seen to the left. (*Ray Whitehouse*)

The Barnett family, *c.* 1902: Abraham and Maria with their children Leonard and Gertrude. Leonard was to become a popular transport provider for many churches and other organisations in Coseley and beyond. (*Stan Barnett*)

An early advertisement for Len Barnett transport. The word 'treats' in the list of options refers to the Sunday school outings, in those times one of the highlights of a child's year. (*Stan Barnett*)

A Barnett charabanc about to take a ladies' outing from Ebenezer Baptist Chapel, *c.* 1927. Len Barnett, the driver, can be seen standing at the front, possibly on the running board, looking straight at the camera. (*Stan Barnett*)

A dashing picture of Len Barnett, the young successful transport operator. (*Margaret Lane*)

Len with his wife Mary in the late 1950s. (*Stan Barnett*)

A Wolverhampton Corporation motor bus standing on Snow Hill, 1953, outside Tweedies Sport, Scouts, and Camping shop, in preparation for its journey to Sedgley via Fighting Cocks. The area where it stands has now been completely cleared and roofed over as part of Wolverhampton's Wulfrun Centre/Mander Centre shopping complex. The motorbuses replaced the once-familiar trolley buses that journeyed from Wolverhampton to Dudley, via Sedgley, providing good access to either town for many years. (*John Hughes*)

The firm of John Thompson, Ettingshall, originally a boilermaker, diversified into many products over the years. This view looking east along Davis Street, no longer a right of way but kept entirely for works' use, shows the motor pressings tool room on the left and the workshops on the right. Many famous chassis frames, for both lorries and cars, including Leyland and Rolls-Royce, were pressed here. (*Trevor Genge*)

Most of the larger firms introduced their own liveried transport vehicles, a tendency now being reversed. Here is a Cannon iron foundries van at the Deepfields site in 1926. (*Frank Jones*)

8

Industry

A new shaft is sunk off Himley Road, 1950. (*John Grainger*)

The Cuba Pit, Lower
Gornal, and its colliers,
c. 1900. Whatever the
dangers of the job, or
how well they were
rewarded, there was
always a wish to be
associated with the place
of work, which these
men clearly indicate.
(*Black Country Society*)

John Thompson Motor Pressings Ltd were situated on the south side of Millfields Road, and therefore entirely within the old bounds of Sedgley. Fittingly they took the Beacon as their logo, including a facsimile of the tower top. (*Stan Barnett*)

John Thompson chassis car frames under construction, 1950s. (*Stan Barnett*)

John Thompson milling department during the Second World War, when the factory turned to wartime production. Note the axles in the foreground. (*Stan Barnett*)

John Thompson aero department was created during the Second World War for wartime needs. Here aero engine cowls are in production. (*Stan Barnett*)

In 1977 the John Thompson Construction and Aero Offices have already been demolished, and workshops will follow them as part of the blight on Black Country heavy industry. (*Trevor Genge*)

In the late 1980s old colliery sites and the land opened up as the result of the demolition of Bilston Steelworks allowed the construction of a new link road with the Black Country Route and the M6. The Sedgemore Park housing estate together with new retail warehouses and light industrial units filled up the rest of the sites. (*F.A. Barnett*)

9

People & Events

A place in the sun in Sedgley for these men sitting at the point where Dudley Street meets the Bull Ring, early 1900s. Could they have been waiting for a tram on a day too pleasant to take advantage of the nearby tram waiting room? (*Chris Lloyd*)

John Lawton, seen here with his wife Hannah in their garden at Spring Road, Lanesfield, where he was a well-known figure. The pleasure gardens next door belong to the Three Cups Inn. There is a glimpse of the old cottages opposite that stood just below the Wesleyan chapel, and the two-storey backhouses to the rear. John Lawton originally came from Ladymoor, where he worked as a blacksmith. This photograph was taken in about 1944. (*Linda Lawton*)

Do you recognise this man? A policeman in training, probably at Mill Meece, Stoke on Trent, in about 1920. (*Matthew Mills*)

Having first been a policeman at Stone, here the same policeman is seen on the beat, somewhere in Coseley, where he became a familiar figure in many parts of this extensive district. (*Matthew Mills*)

Many Coseley people will have recognised Sergeant Horace Thorne, who here, near to retirement, poses for a photograph behind Coseley police station, 1950. He had served in Coseley since 1936. (*Matthew Mills*)

Some of Sedgley's Urban District councillors gather on site, off Bilston Street, to discuss plans for the Greenway area estate, which was to be part of the 'Homes fit for Heroes' scheme, 1920s. (*Diane Turner*)

The entrance to the estate was seen at its best when this picture postcard was produced and sold in local shops. (*Trevor Genge*)

Hurst Hill crossroads. One winter's morning in 2001 a car was found to have skidded on an icy road, demolishing the railings around Dr Baker's statue, and coming to rest against the plinth. (*Jenny Hill*)

Fortunately the damage to the plinth was remedied, and here is Councillor Norman Davies, Wolverhampton MB and leader of the council, together with descendants of Dr Baker, at the ceremony in 2002 marking the statue's restoration. Denys Baker, a grandson, can be seen to the left next to Councillor Davies, with two other grandchildren to his right. The original opening ceremony in 1914 is shown in *Sedgley & District* book 1. (*Jenny Hill*)

At the entry into Gorge Road, Hurst Hill, where the A463 passes through the Silurian limestone cutting, a wall collapsed after heavy and prolonged rain in 2001, reducing the width to single carriageway. Here work is in progress to restore the supporting wall of the higher ground above and reopen the other carriageway. (*Trevor Genge*)

From the garden above the collapsed wall the cause can be seen, to the far right, where the remaining brickwork of an old forgotten well remains intact. (*Trevor Genge*)

Sedgley councillors commence work on the plantation project on the Beacon. The original plan was to plant trees the length of the ridge, but this was not pursued further. This first plantation of 1936 remains, a reminder of their intentions. Left to right: Henry Griffin, Tom Knight, Dan Price, J. Hemmings (with spade), E. Friend, A.E. Dick (surveyor), J.E. Richards, George Mills, H.J. Morris and F. Foster. (*Chris Lloyd*)

A Second World War photograph of a parade by civil defence and ambulance drivers from Zoar Chapel. The Second World War brought a new emphasis on civil defence. Not only did such parades bond different skills together, but it boosted the confidence of the local population both during the war and in the postwar years. Prominent in the front row are Mr Stanley (second from left) and Eustace Cropper (third from left), and also visible are Mrs Udall, Dorothy Hughes, Margaret Cook and Stella Lewis. (*Margaret Cook*)

This was the photograph used by John Ernest Timmins of Lower Gornal for his election address when he first entered local politics, hoping for a seat on Sedgley's Urban District Council. (*Vi Marsh*)

Here, in 1960, John Ernest Timmins (now Chairman of the Sedgley Urban District Council) is seen with his wife Nora, welcoming Dudley's Mayor and Mayoress, Mr and Mrs Preedy. His name can be seen with other local civic leaders on the recently found Sedgley Council Chairman's Boards (see page 116). (*Vi Marsh*)

In addition to his political career, John Timmins became the owner of Matthew Southall, wholesale fruit and vegetable merchants, Dudley; he is seen here at the entrance. (*Vi Marsh*)

Joseph Roper (left), Clerk to Coseley Urban District Council. Standing to his right is Mr Balshaw, the park superintendent, with another associate. Joseph Roper was the father of the solicitor and local historian John Roper, featured in book 4. (*Margaret Roper*)

A reminder of local shops comes with Albert and Lydia Timmins's general store in the Coppice area, which served Upper Ettingshall, Woodsetton and Hurst Hill. The proliferation of advertisements was normal for the 1920s, when this photograph was taken. (*Matthew Mills*)

I.Z. Butler's Fancy Repository, Bull Ring, Sedgley, *c.* 1910. In the late nineteenth century Betsy Butler from Wednesbury ran a drapery store at 1 Bull Ring, and the family continued to run the shop through the next generation. The shop (now a wool shop) is part of a block of four late Georgian houses which still stands. (*Chris Lloyd*)

10

A Walk Around the Heart of Sedgley

The St George's Day Parade involves all local groups of Wolverhampton South District Scout Association, to which Sedgley Scouts belonged. Here the Scouts are marching along Vicar Street, April 1963. The high wall in the Priory and around the side of the old vicarage reveals where the former stable and coach house was. A windowed house gable is seen above. By following their procession we can see the once-familiar buildings of the village in this period. (*George Cox*)

Scouts and Cubs outside the parish church. (*George Cox*)

Marching out of Vicar Street and into Gospel End Street reminds us of the old Seven Stars Inn and the adjacent cottages. (*George Cox*)

The Cubs enter Gospel End Street, passing the old pawn shop. (*George Cox*)

The band leads around the Bull Ring and up Dudley Street. Behind them can be seen Arthur Croyden's barber's shop, the Red Lion Inn, Hartill's butcher's shop and the Sedgley branch of Chapman's the bakers. Chapman's advertise other branches at Bilston and Dudley. Hartill's shop was once occupied by I.Z. Butler (see page 94). (*George Cox*)

The band returns past the parish church and heads for Dean Street. Rain has clearly set in! (*George Cox*)

The long procession of Scouts and Cubs marches around the Bull Ring, while a Wolverhampton trolley bus waits patiently for them to pass. The Clifton cinema can be seen to the left. (*George Cox*)

A reminder of scouting in former years. Here in 1934 the 1st Sedgley Scouts are on parade in a procession, heading for the parish church, along Tipton Street. The occasion is the Sunday school anniversary. (*George Cox*)

11

Epitaph to the Cannon Industries

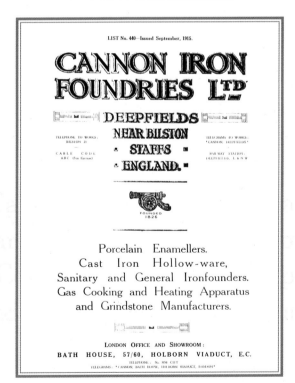

The small foundry begun by Edward and Stephen Sheldon in 1826 became Cannon Iron Foundry, producing a wide range of cast goods. Here is the front page of their 1915 catalogue.

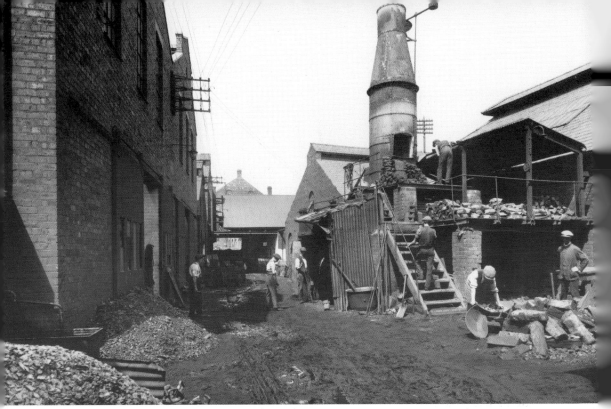

Above: This photograph is one of many taken at the firm in 1926 to celebrate its centenary. Much of what can be seen here is of the original plant of Edward Sheldon. The tall cupola still had to be charged by hand. One man fills his basket, another climbs the stairway. The surrounding roadway was not tarmacked until the 1930s. (*Frank Jones*)

Below: The Cannon, best known today for gas cookers and fires, diversified into many other products. This is the oval pot-moulding shop. Note the unusually shaped moulds being filled – in most foundries these were rectangular – designed to use less sand. (*Frank Jones*)

A small collection of hollowware produced at Cannon, 1915. Note particularly the pit bottom kettles. (*Frank Jones*)

Here is what is thought to be an original building of the Sheldon works, which was soon to be demolished. The Clayton family have been owners of the firm for some years. The canal is the Birmingham Canal navigation main line, and its Cannon arm was indispensable for ease of transport at this time. The heavy goods or containers were loaded into boats from the inside of the works. Part of the Clayton family moved to Tewkesbury, and Talbot Clayton was known for his arrival at work by motor launch! (*Frank Jones*)

Two Cannon products are painted. On the left a ten-section hot-water radiator has its enamel brush-painted, while the traditional gas cooker has most of its body sprayed with black japan. (*Frank Jones*)

Polishing castings. Castings needed polishing to remove blemishes before japanning took place. Here men stand by their polishers turned by the once well-known drive power of belted shafting, the shaft being driven by a single power source. In earlier times a steam engine would have provided the power. In this case the shafting drives the polishers for up to a dozen men. Jim Clarke is the workman in the foreground. (*Frank Jones*)

The assembly shop was a labour-intensive department where all products needing assembly were brought. Some of the men worked an 8½-hour day. In the foreground are the typical Cannon gas cookers of the 1920s and '30s. Tom Porter is the foreman, standing in the centre wearing the flat cap. (*Frank Jones*)

Opposite, top: The large casting shop, with the overhead gantry crane lifting both top and bottom box moulds, which had to remain in line. These moulds were too heavy to lift unaided. (*Frank Jones*)

Opposite: The machine shop shows Tom Jackson drilling the top flange of a cast-iron toilet bowl. Here again the drilling machine is driven from cone pulleys on a common shafting – and note that there are no safety guards by the moving belt! (*Frank Jones*)

Cannon also expanded into making grinding machines. Here the abrasive wheels lie stacked in the open. This photograph also gives a fine view of the adjacent Stour Valley railway line, which served Wolverhampton and Birmingham and beyond, and the cottages in Havacre Lane. Beyond to the west are the unspoilt open fields towards Sedgley Beacon, complete with water tower. Cannon's last department closed in March 2003, putting an end to 177 years of our industrial history. (*Frank Jones*)

Working alone in the tinning shop, an unpleasant job with both fumes and heat, and the need for protection, as evidenced by the long apron.

Edward Sheldon, founder of the firm (his brother Stephen seems to have abandoned the project in the early days).

Richard Clayton, first of the Clayton family to inherit the firm, also became the first Chairman of Coseley Council. He did not live to see the centenary, by which time R. Talbot Clayton was managing director.

PROGRAMME.

SATURDAY.

4th. May.

3-0 p.m.   **OPENING OF THE CLAYTON PLAYING FIELDS by R. D. B. CLAYTON, Esq., of Hardwick Manor, Tewkesbury.**

Chair to be taken by the Chairman of the Council (**Councillor Isaiah Greensill, J.P.**).

The Fields have been presented by the family of the late Alderman Richard Clayton, J.P., the first Chairman of the Coseley Urban District Council, and have been equipped by the Council with Swings, Whirling Platforms, Giant Slides, Sandpit, etc.

A Shelter and Lavatories have also been erected.

SUNDAY.

5th. May.

10-0 a.m.   **CIVIC SUNDAY.** The Chairman of the Council (**Councillor Isaiah Greensill, J.P.**), Members, Officers, Townsmen and Friends assemble at the Council House, and at 10-15 o'clock proceed to the Baptist Church, Princes End, where the annual Civic Service will be conducted by the Rev. T. J. Pennell, Chairman's Chaplain.

Silver Jubilee celebration programme for the opening of the Clayton Playing Fields, 1935. The Clayton family gave the extensive land at the rear of their old home for the creation of a playing field, named Clayton Playing Fields in memory of their father Richard, Coseley Council's first chairman. Coseley Urban District Council provided the swings and other facilities. The opening of the playing fields was arranged to coincide with the Jubilee celebrations, and son Robert performed the initial ceremony.

12

History in the Detail

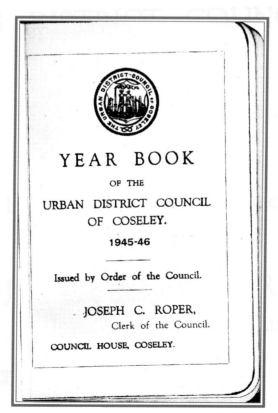

YEAR BOOK

OF THE

URBAN DISTRICT COUNCIL OF COSELEY.

1945-46

Issued by Order of the Council.

JOSEPH C. ROPER,
Clerk of the Council.

COUNCIL HOUSE, COSELEY.

Coseley Urban District Council Year Book, 1945–6.

PROGRAMME.

MONDAY.

6th. May.

5-0 p.m.   **Old Folk's Jubilee Tea** at Mount Pleasant Schools.

Old Age Pensioners of seventy years and upwards are being entertained by the Council.

10-0 p.m.   **Boy Scout Beacon Chain—**

Beacon Fire to be lit on Sedgley Beacon, Coseley.

Illuminations and Decorations.

The Green at Old End will be decorated and illuminated, and it is hoped that Tradespeople will decorate their premises during the celebrations.

The 1935 Jubilee celebrations included tea parties, a chain of beacons (including Sedgley's) and decorations and illuminations.

COUNCIL OFFICIALS

Name.	Office.	Date of Appointment.
CLERK'S DEPARTMENT :—		
JOSEPH CHARLES ROPER	Clerk of the Council : Returning Officer at Elections ; Clerk to the Rating Authority ; Clerk to the Old Age Pension Committee; Registrar of Local Land Charges ; National Registration and Food Executive Officer.	3rd December, 1925.
ALBERT EDWARD .WEBB	Chief Clerk	4th July, 1941.
MAUD LYONS	Secretary Typist	8th June, 1931.
KATHLEEN SKELDING	Shorthand Typist (on Service)	5th July, 1937.
MONA STRETTON SPEAKE	Housing Assistant	26th October, 1942.
VIOLET IRENE FLAVELL	Shorthand Typist (Temporary)	9th December, 1940.
BESSIE BARBARA HALE	Switchboard Operator	27th January, 1943.
FINANCE DEPARTMENT :—		
HOWARD JOSHUA JONES	Treasurer (Barclay's Bank)	12th March, 1940.
WILLIAM ERNEST WHITE	Accountant and Chief Financial Officer.	10th December, 1929.
FRANK ERNEST PRICE	Rating and Valuation Officer	2nd April, 1912.
CHARLES HARRISON	Collector.	1st June, 1938.
JOSEPH DEAKIN	Rent Collector	23rd March, 1926.
HAROLD BRADLEY	Rent Collector (on Service)	5th June, 1939.
JOHN WILSON	Rent Collector	10th June, 1940.
ELIZABETH LLOYD	Accounts Clerk (Temporary)	7th May, 1942.
DOROTHY JEAN EASTHOPE	Shorthand Typist	26th May, 1942.

COUNCIL OFFICIALS—*continued*.

Name.	Office.	Date of Appointment.
HEALTH DEPARTMENT :—		
ALEXANDER JOSEPH WATT	Medical Officer of Health and School Medical Officer	20th September, 1938.
JANE ANGELA NAGLE	Medical Officer—Ante-natal Clinic	1st January, 1938.
WILLIAM GEORGE WEBSTER	Dental Surgeon.	27th October, 1936.
GEORGE HORACE PARKES	Chief Sanitary Inspector, Inspector of Factories and Workshops.	10th January, 1928.
RAYMOND BRUCE ANDERSON	Additional Sanitary Inspector	28th June, 1945.
TRYPHENA NICHOLSON	Health Visitor	6th October, 1931.
MARGARET ELIZABETH GIBSON	Health Visitor	4th April, 1938.
ETHEL BURGESS	Shorthand Typist	20th September, 1937.
JEAN PARKES	General Clerk	24th May, 1943.
MOLLY MOORHOUSE	Matron—War Time Nursery	12th July, 1943.
DORA BRAWN	Assistant Matron—War Time Nursery.	1st January, 1945.
SURVEYOR'S DEPARTMENT :—		
PHILIP JAMES STANTON	Surveyor	11th June, 1945.
EDWARD J. H. BONUGLI	Junior Engineering Assistant (on Service).	14th August, 1939.
NEVILLE ASTON	Junior Draughtsman	28th February, 1944.
DOROTHY ISABEL HICKMAN	Shorthand Typist	15th May, 1942.
DAVID MITCHELL	Clerk of Works	13th August, 1945.
JAMES BERNARD TEDESCHI	Sewage Works Manager	15th May, 1945

This list of council officers provides a reminder of both names and services in the years 1945–6.

Sedgley Local History Society & Museum

Details of boards in Sedgley Council House showing Chairmen/women.   The earliest dates are from the establishment of the Upper Board, and before the Sedgley UDC was formed.

Rev. William Lewis	1867 – 69		James P. Fithern	1955
The Hon. Rev. Adelbert Anson	1870 – 72		Frederick S. Dews	1956
John Barrs	1873		Cyril Caddick	1957
Joseph Low	1873		Mrs Ethel E. Williams	1958
Frederick A. Homer	1874		Joseph Jones O.B.E.	1959
Robert Orman	1875		John E. Timmins	1960
Dr. Eagleton	1876		Thomas P. Hanley	1961
Frederick A. Homer	1877-78		Allan J. R. Hickling	1962
Stephen Wilkes	1879		Albert Oakley	1963
John Hughes	1880-81		Alban H. Jones	1964
Stephen Wilkes	1882-94		Charles A. Turner	1965
(UDC) Stephen Wilkes	1895-96		(End of the Sedgley UDC)	
John Hughes	1897-98			
John Twigg Homer	1899-00			
William E. Fithern	1901			
William A Foster	1902			
John T. Tennant	1903-04			
William E. Fithern	1905-06			
William H. Haden	1907-08			
Leonard Foster	1909-11			
John T. Tennant	1912			
Alfred H. Pearcey	1913-15			
Thomas Southall	1916			
Joseph Brown	1917			
Thomas Southall	1918			
Joseph Brown	1919-20			
William F. Dews	1921-24			
Charles A. Pratt	1925-29			
William F, Dews	1930			
George Mills	1931-33			
John H. Hemmings	1934-36			
George Mills	1937			
John H. Hemmings	1938-42			
D. Ronald Marsh	1943			
Charles A. Pratt	1944		THE "LOST" BOARDS WERE FOUND BY:	
Stephen Bagley	1945		JOHN HEMINGWAY (DUDLEY M. B. ARCHAEOLOGIST)	
Charles Wittingham	1946		GEORGE BLACKHAM & TREVOR GENGE (S. L.H.S)	
Benjamin Timmins	1947		ON MONDAY 29TH APRIL 2002. IN A ROOF ROOM.	
William P. Booth	1948			
Joseph Jones	1949			
Jabez Fellows	1950			
Ethel E. Williams	1951			
George Harrison	1952			
Major Jones	1953			
L. M. Aston	1954		TRANSCRIBED BY TREVOR GENGE 30-04-2002	

Sedgley Urban District Council boards containing lists of past chairmen. These boards were thought lost when the building ceased to be used. Happily, they were found again on 29 April 2002, and now hang in Sedgley Community Centre. This is a transcript on behalf of the Sedgley Local History Society and Museum. The first eleven officers named were chairmen of the Sedgley Upper Board before the coming of the urban district councils.

Every wall tells its own story. Sedgley's walls are traditionally of Gornal stone, with triangular capstones, but there are variations. Here, in 1975, at Darkhouse Cemetery, Coseley, the wall has been built from local furnace waste (or clinker,) but a Gornal stone cap has been added. (*Trevor Genge*)

A rare drystone wall in Lower Gornal, early 1970s. This was probably built from the less plentiful, but local, supply of red sandstone present in the Gordon's Place area of the Straits. (*F.A. Barnett*)

On the corner of Portland Place and Mason Street, Coseley, stands the Hop & Barleycorn, which is near the original site but very different from the former house of that name (which can be seen in book 2, page 76).

The wide openness of the area, and the accesses from Oak Street, Mason Street (Chad Road is a modern name), Providence Row and Portland Place show the expanse of Coseley's own bull-baiting ring. (*Trevor Genge*)

In Upper Gornal an old stone stile post stands against a damaged wall, a reminder of an ancient way into fields, 1940. Sadly the post has now been lost, but the picture remains as evidence. (*Trevor Genge*)

For the Silver Jubilee of Queen Elizabeth II in 1977 traditional street parties took place around the area. This snapshot of a party at Woodcross provides a pleasant reminder of the occasion. (*Matthew Mills*)

This early 1970s photograph of cottages on either side of the first Primitive Methodist Chapel, in Gospel End Street, has now seen much change. The cottage on the right has long been demolished and the chapel recently converted into dwellings, and others to the left refurbished. But the date stone remains on the former chapel, revealing its foundation as being in 1821. (*Trevor Genge*)

How long will the old building that shares a stone wall with Ruiton Congregational Church graveyard remain? While it is supposed to have had various uses over the years, it was certainly used by Ruiton salt sellers to store salt. (*Trevor Genge*)

The building at the bottom of Hall Street, Sedgley, seen here in 1949 and now part of the Sedgley Conservative Club, was obviously not a dwelling as the cottages on page 121 once were. With reinforcement bars it is known to have been both a workshop and, at one time, an abattoir. (*Trevor Genge*)

An intriguing stone in the wall of the Hall Street building begs the question who possessed those initials and claimed to be its builders in August 1812? (*Trevor Genge*)

Gospel End Street, Sedgley, near the Bull Ring, showing an accumulation of buildings with the cottages along the old footpath to All Saints' Church, and the adjacent houses of Pope's Row at right angles to them. One can readily imagine the density of the former community around the parish church, and the density of houses at this point, remembering the demolished cottages on both sides of the road, and on Dean Street. Here in 2000 we see a glimpse of a past where little seems to have changed. (*Trevor Genge*)

The importance of artist historians is not to be forgotten, especially where they illustrate local historical events. Ron Baker has here captured an element of Ruiton under the title Botany Bay. Botany was an area of Ruiton where people worked hard and long in the nailing trade, and with meagre rewards. Ruiton folk must

have thought it quite appropriate to name the area after the notorious penal colony in the southern hemisphere.

A twentieth-century reminder of local history in the parish of Sedgley, *c.* 1940. Andrew Barnett stands in a stubble field behind the recently built Hill Avenue Primary School, with a scholar, Tommy Phillips, who is no doubt being given an introduction to the past. (*Mavis Davies*)

ACKNOWLEDGEMENTS

T he author acknowledges his gratitude to the many people who have provided either pictures or information used in this book. Every effort has been made to contact copyright holders of photographs where copyright has not originated with the person owning them. The Cannon centenary photographs can be attributed to G. Marshall Smith of London.

Thanks are due also to the National Museum of Photography, Film & Television in Bradford; the London Transport Museum; the *Wolverhampton Express & Star*, the Black Country Society; the Dudley Archives and Local History Centre; Lanesfield Primary School and COLAB Birmingham.

My thanks go also to Ron Baker and Margaret Roper, for their usual support and interest. I have also drawn from the work of the late Andrew Barnett, John Roper, Richard Dews, Richard Dews, John Grainger, E. Faulks and Ann Stansfield.

For their contributions, either in photographs, information, or both, I thank George Cox, Frank and Kit Jones, David Melhuish, Ann Hill, Jenny Hill, Jean Darlington, Colin Hale, Ian Beach, Ron Williams, Gwen Green, Brian Gelsthorpe, Alec Martin, Mary and Laurence Nickolds, Stan Barnett, Vi. Marsh, Margaret Cook, Doreen Thompson, Lyn Suvanto (Canada), Linda Lawton, Ray Whitehouse, John Hughes, Gladys Thomas, Alan Malpass, Matthew Mills, Cecil and Dorothy Baines, Margaret Genge, Flo Edwards, Diane Turner, Christine Buckley, Christopher Lloyd, Iris Turley, Gary Barton, Mavis Davies, Fran Plane and Margaret Lane. Other photographs are from the author's collection.

THE BLACK COUNTRY SOCIETY

The Black Country Society is proud to be associated with **Sutton Publishing** of Stroud. In 1994 the society was invited by Sutton Publishing to collaborate in what has proved to be a highly successful publishing partnership, namely the extension of the **Britain in Old Photographs** series into the Black Country. In this joint venture the Black Country Society has played an important role in establishing and developing a major contribution to the region's photographic archives by encouraging society members to compile books of photographs of the area or town in which they live.

The first book in the Black Country series was *Wednesbury in Old Photographs* by Ian Bott, launched by Lord Archer of Sandwell in November 1994. Since then 55 Black Country titles have been published. The total number of photographs contained in these books is in excess of 11,000, suggesting that the whole collection is probably the largest regional photographic survey of its type in any part of the country to date.

This voluntary society, affiliated to the Civic Trust, was founded in 1967 as a reaction to the trends of the late 1950s and early '60s. This was a time when the reorganisation of local government was seen as a threat to the identity of individual communities and when, in the name of progress and modernisation, the industrial heritage of the Black Country was in danger of being swept away.

The general aims of the society are to stimulate interest in the past, present and future of the Black Country, and to secure at regional and national levels an accurate understanding and portrayal of what constitutes the Black Country and, wherever possible, to encourage and facilitate the preservation of the Black Country's heritage.

The society, which now has over 2,500 members worldwide, organises a yearly programme of activities. There are six venues in the Black Country where evening meetings are held on a monthly basis from September to April. In the summer months, there are fortnightly guided evening walks in the Black Country and its green borderland, and there is also a full programme of excursions further afield by car. Details of all these activities are to be found on the society's website, **www.blackcountrysociety.co.uk**, and in *The Blackcountryman*, the quarterly magazine that is distributed to all members.

PO Box 71 · Kingswinford · West Midlands DY6 9YN